Taking care of your

PARAKEET

A Young Pet Owner's Guide
by Helen Piers

Consulting Editor: Matthew M. Vriends, Ph.D.

BARRON'S

First edition for the United States and Canada
published 1993 by Barron's Educational Series, Inc.

First published in Great Britain in 1993 by
Frances Lincoln Limited, 4 Torriano Mews
Torriano Avenue, London NW5 2RZ

All inquiries should be addressed to:
Barron's Educational Series, Inc.
250 Wireless Boulevard
Hauppauge, NY 11788

Library of Congress Catalog Card No. 93-16977

International Standard Book No. 0-8120-1370-0

Library of Congress Cataloging-in-Publication Data
Available upon request

Printed and bound in Hong Kong

3 4 5 6   9 8 7 6 5 4 3 2 1

Contents

Parakeets as pets

Parakeets (also called budgerigars – budgies for short) are a species of small parrot. They were first brought to Europe from Australia about 150 years ago, and they have adapted so well to living in captivity and proved so easy to tame that nowadays many millions of them are kept as pets all over the world.

These cheerful, intelligent little birds are not difficult to look after, and they are inexpensive to feed. But what really makes budgies such good pets is the way they enjoy human company, and take an interest in everything that is going on around them.

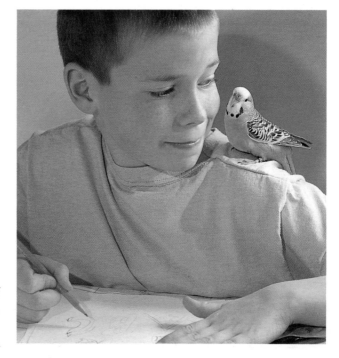

A tame parakeet becomes very attached to its owner. It will come when called and sometimes even preen (groom) its owner's hair as if he or she were another bird. Some parakeets can also learn to talk.

Wild parakeets are found in the semi-desert lands of central Australia. They are nomadic birds, which live in large flocks. Always on the move in search of water to drink and seeding grasses on which to feed, a flock of parakeets will often fly many miles in one day. In the summer when it becomes too hot for them and food is particularly scarce, they migrate to the south of the continent, where it is cooler.

Parakeets never build nests and they do not return each year to the same breeding places to rear their young, as many other birds do. Wherever they happen to be, they find sheltered and convenient places, like the hollows of trees or cavities in rocks, in which to lay their eggs.

Wild parakeets are light green, with yellow head, shoulders, and wings. But pet parakeets are bred in different shades of green, blue, mauve, yellow, and white. *Pied* parakeets have bands or patches of a second color.

There are also *crested* parakeets.

Is a parakeet the right pet?

A parakeet kept on its own needs a lot of human company, or it will be lonely. If it has to be left all by itself for several hours at a time, it is a good idea to leave the radio on. Tune it to a station that features a lot of talking.

There are some things you should think about before you decide to buy a parakeet.

Will you keep one bird or a pair?

It is natural for parakeets to live in flocks, as they do in the wild, so if one is kept on its own it is likely to be very lonely. It will usually adopt its owner as a companion to take the place of other birds, but only if he or she can spend a lot of time with it, talking to it, and taking it out to play. If left alone too much, a parakeet may become ill.

If you will not have time to give your budgie the attention a single bird needs, or if it will be left alone all day when the whole family is out, it would be kinder to keep a pair. It is often believed that parakeets kept in pairs never become tame because they have each other and do not need human company so much. But this does not have to be the case. If you have the time and patience, it is possible to keep two birds separately until they are tame, and only then put them together in the same cage (see page 16).

Will your parents or someone else in the family help you?

There will be times when you are too busy to look after and entertain your budgie, so it is important that someone else in the family is ready to help out. You will also need to plan for vacations. Do you have a friend who will look after your budgie if you go away?

Will your parakeet get enough exercise?

Pet parakeets do not have to fly for miles in search of food, because their food is brought to them. Even so, they need to exercise their wings, and are not really happy or healthy unless they are let out of their cage for at least an hour every day and allowed to fly freely around the room.

Do you have a cat or a dog?

Keeping a parakeet in the same house as a cat is very difficult. It is a cat's natural instinct to hunt birds, and a parakeet flying around the room is easy prey. But an obedient dog will sometimes accept a bird as part of the family, and not harm it.

Parakeets are active, intelligent birds, and easily get bored, so it is important to provide them with toys. This parakeet has learned to climb the ladder and ring the bell at the top.

If you have more than one budgie, they may never be as tame as a single bird, but it can be very interesting watching how they behave together. They will usually preen each other and sometimes you will see one bowing its head for the other one to scratch.

Things you will need

Checklist

- cage
- sheets of sandpaper
- gravel or corn cob litter
- feeding dishes
- water bottle
- perches
- perch brush
- food:
  seed mixture
  green vegetables
- millet spray
- cuttlefish bone
- mineral block
- grit
- clips for fixing cuttle-fish bone and millet spray to cage bars
- vitamins
- mite spray
- toys

A cage.

Sheets of sandpaper and gravel for the floor of the cage (see NEVER box).

The cage will come supplied with perches made of wood or hard plastic. However, you should put in some natural branches as well – these are uneven, so the bird is less likely to get cramps or sores on its toes through always gripping with its feet in the same position (see NEVER box).

8

Transparent feeding dishes are best. The budgie can see the seed inside and find it more easily. You will need two small dishes for seeds and grit, and a larger one for greens and fruit.

Food (see checklist and page 18).

Water bottle.

Millet spray.

Vitamins.

Cuttlefish bone and clip.

Grit.

Mineral block.

Perch brush.

Toys.

Mite spray.

Never

For the cage floor
If you do not use sandpaper you can put a sheet of newspaper under a layer of gravel, but *never* if it is printed in color as it may be poisonous.
For perches
Never use wood from yew trees — it is poisonous. Branches from fruit trees are best.

Grit should be flint or granite grit, or sea sand, mixed with oyster grit (but not white sand, sold for canaries).

A parakeet easily gets bored if it has the same toys all the time, so collect quite a few and put them in the cage in rotation. A mirror helps a single bird feel less lonely. Watching its own reflection, it probably thinks there is another bird in the cage.

9

The cage

Choose the biggest cage you can afford and have room for. The ideal size for two parakeets is about 36 × 18 inches (91 × 45 cm) and 18 inches (45 cm) high, and about two-thirds that size for a single bird.

Pet stores sell bird cages, or you may find one secondhand. There are many different types of cages to choose from, and it is worthwhile looking around to find the best. The cage is going to be your parakeet's home for its whole life, so it is important to select one in which your pet will be comfortable and happy.

Important points about the cage

Is it big enough?

Is it the right shape? A tall circular cage looks attractive, but does not give a bird enough space to stretch its wings.

Does the door fasten securely?

The cage should have a molded plastic tray at the bottom that slides out to make cleaning easy.

The bars of the cage can be chromium plated or enameled metal. Choose a cage that has at least some horizontal bars, rather than all vertical, so that your budgie can use them as a climbing frame.

Where should the cage be kept?

Parakeets need company. Yours will be happier in a room where the family spends a lot of time. Choose a room where you can safely let your pet out of its cage to fly about. Parakeets need plenty of air, so the room should never be allowed to get too stuffy. A kitchen is not suitable because of cooking fumes.

Do you need a stand for the cage?

This is not essential. The cage can sit on any firm table or shelf. However, a cage on a stand takes up less space. It is also easier to move about, and is raised up high, which birds prefer.

Never

Never keep the cage in a draft, and *never* by a hot radiator or near a smoky fire.

Never keep it in the kitchen – cooking fumes are harmful and there are too many dangers for a bird flying about outside its cage (see page 22).

Never keep it directly in front of a window. It is much too cold in winter and too hot in summer.

Parakeets can suffer stress through lack of sleep. So cover the cage with a light cloth in the evening. This should subdue the light, but not leave the bird in total darkness. (Make sure your pet will have enough air!)

Buying a parakeet

On some young parakeets (like the one above) the stripy head markings extend across the forehead and down to the cere. These disappear after the first molt at three months.

Most pet stores sell parakeets, or you may be able to buy one directly from a breeder. Bird farms advertise in bird magazines.

Take your time when choosing your pet. Watch for the ones that are more lively and active and take more interest in you when you go near the cage. A bird's color will make no difference to its temperament or whether it will be easier to tame.

You will have to trust the breeder or pet store assistant to know whether a young bird is a cock (male) or a hen (female), because only an expert can tell at this stage.

How old should the parakeet be?

The younger the better. By six months old a parakeet is very difficult to tame. Six weeks is the best age, unless the bird has already been tamed by the breeder.

How can you tell how old a parakeet is?

A six-week-old's beak may be dark or mottled, and when under three months its *cere* (the waxy swelling above the beak) is light pink, not blue or brown as in adults (see opposite).

Which sex make the best pets?

Cocks and hens make equally good pets. **Two cocks** or **two hens** can be kept in the same cage, or **one hen** and **one** or **two cocks**. But *two hens and one cock can never be kept together* because the hens will fight.

How do you know if a parakeet is healthy?

Its feathers should be smooth and sleek, not spiky, and not fluffed up unless it is sleeping.

Its tail and wing feathers should not be bent or sticking out at angles.

Its breast should be well-rounded, not hollow.

Its cere should be clean, without crustiness.

Its eyes should be bright, and not runny.

It should breathe with its beak closed.

Telling a cock from a hen
The cere of an adult cock (above) is bright blue, and a hen's (below) is beige to brown. (Exceptions are the *Pied* and *Lutino* parakeets, both sexes of which have fleshy pink ceres.)

You will probably be given your bird in a cardboard box. Carry the box in your hands to avoid it getting jostled, and make your journey home as short as possible. If the weather is cold, wrap a scarf loosely around the box or hold it under your coat, but make sure the parakeet gets enough air.

Getting the cage ready

If possible, prepare the cage before you go out to buy your parakeet (or pair of parakeets, if you have decided to keep two).

First, wash the whole cage in very hot water. Do not use soap or detergent, and only use disinfectant if it is the kind sold especially for bird cages. If you use a secondhand cage, you *must* disinfect it.

Dry the cage thoroughly.

Lay a sheet of sandpaper on the cage floor, and cover it with a sprinkling of gravel. Then arrange the perches, the dishes for seed and grit, and the water bottle. The cuttlefish bone, millet spray, and mineral block should be clipped to the bars of the cage.

Perches should be arranged so that there is one within easy reach of each food dish and the water bottle, and another higher in the cage. They should not be so close to the side of the cage that when the parakeet perches on them its tail rubs against the bars.

To put your budgie into its cage, gently unfasten one end of the carrying box. Then hold the box just inside the open door of the cage, taking care not to leave a space through which the parakeet can escape if it suddenly panics. If it does not hop out at once, you can tilt the box a little.

The first few weeks

Once your parakeet is safely in its cage, it is best to leave it quiet and by itself in the room for two or three hours.

Parakeets are brave little birds, but even so, your new budgie will find everything very unfamiliar and even frightening, and it may be homesick. So for the first week or two it is very important to make sure it is not alarmed by loud noises, or anything else that might be stressful (see NEVER box). Take care that the cage does not face the TV and is not near a harsh light, but avoid leaving your budgie in complete darkness. At night there should be some form of dim light in the room.

If you have bought two parakeets they will be more confident. Even so, you should keep things as calm and quiet as you can.

Sometimes it takes a while for a young parakeet to find the seed inside a seed dish, so it is a good idea to sprinkle a little on the cage floor until you know for sure that it is eating from the dish. Remember, parakeets need to eat little but often.

At first, when you clean the cage or bring food to your new budgie it will probably show alarm. Reassure it by talking softly all the time, and move quietly and gently. When it no longer retreats into a corner or flutters about, and perhaps begins to show interest in what you are doing, then you will know it is feeling at home, and you can begin taming it.

Never

Especially during the first week or two:
Never shout loudly, slam doors, or have the TV or radio on too loud.
Never leave windows wide open onto a street. Cars and sirens may alarm your bird.
Never make sudden movements near the cage, or approach it suddenly.
Never press your face against the bars.

Once you see your budgie pecking at its food, you will know it is beginning to feel less strange in its new home.

- Don't overtire your budgie. Taming sessions should be short (ten minutes), but frequent – even at two-hourly intervals.
- Try not to make sudden movements.
- Do not lift your budgie out of its cage until you are sure it really trusts you, and shows no sign of fear.
- Before you attempt to let your budgie out of its cage make sure the room is escape-proof and safe (see page 22).

All the time and patience you spend on taming your budgie will seem well worthwhile when at last it comes to your hand in answer to its name.

Taming

To tame your budgie you will need to overcome its fear and win its trust. This may take some weeks, so be patient. Follow the method opposite and remember to be gentle and talk soothingly at the same time.

It is best if only one person tries to tame a parakeet. If the whole family takes turns, your bird may get confused. No one else should be in the room during taming, and the TV or radio should be switched off.

If you are keeping two birds together you should be able to win their trust by using the same method, although they will probably never become as tame as a single bird.

If you have started off with one parakeet, you may feel later that it would be happier with a companion. If you decide to buy a second parakeet, and your first bird is already tame, it is a good idea to tame the second bird before you put them together.

You will need to keep the new bird in a separate room until it is tame, and let the two birds get to know each other gradually. First, you can put their cages in the same room. Then, after a week or so, you can let them fly about the room together. But watch carefully, and only put them in the same cage when you are sure they are going to be friends.

In this way you will have two parakeets that are both tame, and yet will never be lonely.

1. To teach your parakeet not to fear your hand, begin by offering it a piece of millet through the cage door. Hold the millet so the bird can reach it, but keep your hand below its head and not too close. It may retreat into a corner or flutter about in alarm. But keep your hand there for a few minutes.

2. Offer the millet frequently, even every two or three hours. After a few days your bird should overcome its fear and begin to peck at it. Then move your hand closer so it has to hop on to your finger to reach the millet. When it does, take care not to jerk your hand in the excitement.

3. When your pet has lost its fear of your hand you can offer your forefinger to it as a perch (without the millet). Press the finger gently against the bird's lower breast, and encourage it by talking softly to it, and saying its name. Be patient – parakeets are very suspicious of anything new.

4. When your parakeet has begun to hop confidently onto your finger you can gently lift it out of the cage. It is important to finger-tame your pet before you let it out to fly around the room. Catching a bird that does not come to your finger is not easy, and can be frightening for the bird.

Feeding 1

Parakeets feed on the seeds of grasses, some fresh greens, and a little fruit.

Seeds

Pet stores sell packeted seeds specially mixed to give parakeets a balanced diet. Make sure the packet is labeled "parakeet seed" – not just "bird seed."

It is important that the seed is fresh. So only buy enough for two months at a time and never store it in a plastic bag – it needs air, or it will become moldy. Seed is best stored in a cloth bag, or in a closed tin *with air holes punched in the lid*, and kept in a cool dry place.

Take care your budgie is never left without seeds to eat. Budgies only eat the kernels, leaving the husks to pile up. You may think the dish is full of seeds, when it is only full of husks.

endive

chickweed

parsley

young dandelion leaves

watercress

spinach

groundsel

These are some of the vegetables and green plants you can give to parakeets. They may also like lettuce, eggplant, green peas, carrots, beets, sweet potatoes, zucchini, and curly kale. Only give lettuce in small amounts.

18

Greens and fruit

At first your parakeet may not touch any greens or fruit. It may never have been given fresh food before. Continue to put some out just the same. In time your bird will pluck up courage and try it, and you will find out which foods it likes best. Do not give too much fruit. A small piece every two days is enough.

Extra foods

During winter and when birds are molting or breeding they need extra nourishment, and enjoy occasional treats of wheat germ, oats, or sunflower seeds. Once a week you can give your parakeet a teaspoon of hard-boiled egg mixed with cottage cheese.

Your pet will enjoy pecking at a millet spray as a treat. This is also very nutritious food. But millet is fattening, so only give about 2 inches (5 cm) of spray a day.

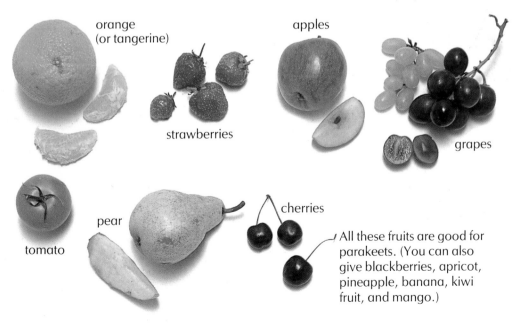

orange (or tangerine)

strawberries

apples

grapes

tomato

pear

cherries

All these fruits are good for parakeets. (You can also give blackberries, apricot, pineapple, banana, kiwi fruit, and mango.)

By pecking at a cuttlefish bone, a parakeet sharpens its beak as well as getting the calcium it needs.
It has a curved beak, specially shaped for taking the husks off seeds.

Vitamins

To make sure your parakeet remains healthy, it is very important to add vitamins (sold at pet stores) to its drinking water.

Cuttlefish bone and mineral block

Pecking at a cuttlefish bone gives a parakeet valuable calcium, and a mineral block provides all the minerals it needs. Both can be clipped to the bars of the cage.

If you buy a cuttlefish bone from the pet store it will already be prepared. But if you pick one up on the beach you will need to clean it. Boil it for one hour, then leave it to soak for a week, changing the water daily.

Grit

Birds have no teeth so they have to swallow grit of some kind to help grind up the food in their gizzard (part of a bird's stomach). Some grit should always be available, either in a dish or sprinkled on the cage floor.

How much food and how often?

How much food a parakeet needs depends on its age, how much exercise it is getting, and its own individual appetite. The important thing is to make sure there is always some food in the cage, because parakeets need to eat little but often. Follow the plan opposite and you will know you are giving your bird enough food. Parakeets rarely overeat unless they are very bored and lonely.

Feeding Plan
In the morning
Clean out the seed dish and fill with seed. Give fresh drinking water.

Two or three times during the day
Remove empty husks from the seed dish (you can blow them off or remove with a small spoon) and fill with fresh seed. If you are going to be out all day it is best to leave two dishes of seed as a parakeet will often go hungry because it cannot find the uneaten seeds hidden under empty husks.

Every other day
Give a small handful of greens and a piece of fruit.

Never

Never give kitchen scraps or chocolate.
Never let the seed become moldy.
Never give frozen, cooked, or canned vegetables and fruit.
Never give fruit or vegetables straight from the refrigerator – all food should be at room temperature.
Never gather plants from beside a road, because of pollution.

You can give fresh food in a dish or poke it through the bars of the cage for the parakeet to peck at.

Flying outside the cage

Once your parakeet is tame you should let it fly outside its cage as much as possible – for at least an hour a day.

Is the room escape-proof?

Make sure all doors and windows are shut *completely*. Parakeets can fly through very narrow gaps. They can also hurt themselves trying to fly through closed windows, because they cannot see the glass. So windows should be curtained or covered in some way. (For other dangers, see the REMEMBER box.)

The first flight outside the cage

The cage will have become the place where your budgie feels safe, and it may be afraid to come out and explore the room. So first lift it out on your finger. Let it perch on top of the cage to look around and decide when it feels safe enough to fly about. Eventually it will take off, fly around the room, and probably settle somewhere high up. It may stay up there a long time, panting with agitation, because leaving its cage for the first time is a big adventure for a young bird. Talk to it reassuringly, but do not try to persuade it to come down.

Your parakeet may be unable to find its way back to its cage, or be too frightened to make the return flight. You can help by lifting the cage up closer to it. But you may have to wait until hunger gives the bird enough courage to return by itself.

Never try to shoo your parakeet back to its cage by waving things at it. Avoid giving it food outside the cage, or it may not be so ready to fly back in. In an emergency, the best way to catch a parakeet is to throw a small piece of lightweight cloth over it, then very gently pick it up with your hands over its *closed* wings.

Will the parakeet do any damage?

It might peck at the wallpaper or books. If it does, you can pin paper over any piece of wall close to the places where it likes to perch, and cover bookcases temporarily with a cloth. Parakeet droppings do not stain, and when dry they can be vacuumed up.

You can make a special perching place for your budgie, using small branches and bamboo. Train an indoor plant to climb up and over them; then hang them with toys. But avoid using any poisonous plants (see REMEMBER box).

The more you play with your budgie, the more friendly it will become. You can train it to climb ropes, ring bells, and roll plastic balls or marbles about – it will enjoy rolling them off the table for you to pick up.

Cleaning

It is important to keep the cage very clean if your parakeet is to stay healthy and be free from parasites.

Once a day
Wash seed dishes in hot water, and dry well before refilling. Remove husks, droppings, and uneaten food from the floor tray. Wipe perches and bars of the cage with a damp (not wet) cloth.

Once a week
Empty the floor tray and wash in very hot water. *Dry it well.* Put in fresh sandpaper or gravel. Scrub perches, and if worn smooth, rub over with coarse sandpaper to roughen them. Wash toys and ladders.

Once a month
Scrub out the whole cage with very hot water. *Rinse and dry well.* **Never** use soap or detergent. Spray with mite spray (from the pet store).

Cleaning is best done during the parakeet's free flight time. The cage (*and the perches*) must be thoroughly dry before the bird returns to it.

Preening and bathing

A parakeet keeps its feathers clean and in good condition by preening, and it can do this better if its feathers are *slightly* damp.

Once every two days, you can give your pet a saucer of lukewarm water – no more than ¾ inch (2 cm) deep – to splash in. Alternatively, you can spray your bird *lightly*. Use a plant sprayer, but make sure it produces a fine spray, not a jet of water.

Only give bath water or spray before midday, so your bird's feathers will be dry by evening. Keep it out of drafts while it is still damp.

Do not give your bird either bath water or spray in very cold weather.

You can buy a bird bath to fix across the open cage door. A sprig of parsley in the water encourages the bird to use it.

A parakeet preens itself by pulling each tail and wing feather through its beak to remove dust and dirt, and by pecking and smoothing down its soft feathers.

Health and illness

Remember

You will help your budgies stay healthy if you:
- Give them a good variety of fresh green food.
- Give extra vitamins, calcium, and minerals (see page 20).
- Keep them out of drafts, and do not let them get too hot or too cold.
- Make sure they get sunshine, but *not* hot midday sun, especially through glass.
- Never let them get lonely or bored.
- Keep the cage clean.

Parakeets rarely get ill, but when they do, they quickly lose condition, so never put off getting help from a veterinarian.

How do you know if a parakeet is ill?

Aside from the symptoms given on the next page, a sick parakeet will take no interest in what is going on, and its eyes will be dull. It will sit low on its perch, huddled up, with feathers fluffed out. It may not be interested in its food, and be more thirsty than usual.

What do you do if your parakeet is ill?

There is some advice on the next page. But it is hard to be sure what is the matter with a bird, so it is best to phone the veterinarian's office and describe your bird's symptoms. The veterinarian will advise you what to do.

Meanwhile make sure your bird is in a quiet, warm place, and has water to drink.

Often a parakeet's beak and claws grow too long. If this happens your veterinarian will clip them painlessly. Do not try to do this yourself.

If your bird has an accident and breaks a leg or a wing it is better to take it to the veterinarian, rather than try to treat it yourself.

Symptoms	Possible cause and what to do
Loss of feathers	All birds *molt* – shed their old feathers and grow new ones – from time to time. Baby parakeets molt at three months, and adults some time during summer or autumn. But if your bird has bald patches, **take it to the veterinarian**. It could have *red mites* or some other parasite. If it continually plucks out feathers, then it may be lonely, or have an *allergy*.
A whitish gray crust appears on the beak and gradually spreads to the cere, around the eyes and on the feet	This is *scaly face*, and is caused by a tiny parasite. The bird should be isolated from other birds, because scaly face is catching. The veterinarian will give you a lotion with which to treat it.
Breathing with the beak open, discharge from the nostrils, rattling throat noises	The parakeet has a cold, or maybe a more serious respiratory infection. **Take it to the veterinarian at once**, but take care to cover the cage or carrying box so it does not get cold.
The droppings are runny and discolored	The bird has *diarrhea*. Maybe it has eaten something that did not agree with it, but diarrhea can be a sign of a more serious illness, so keep the bird warm, remove green food, and **telephone your veterinarian**.
The bird is straining as if it is having trouble passing its droppings	It may be *constipated*. Give extra green food. If no better in 24 hours **take it to the vet**. But if it is a *hen bird* and seems in pain, she may be having difficulty laying an egg. This could be serious, **so take her to the veterinarian at once**. (Hens lay eggs even if they have no mate.)

Breeding parakeets

Parakeets will not breed unless they have a nesting box. Pet stores sell them, or you can make your own. The box should be about 6 × 9½ inches (15 × 24 cm) and 5½ inches (14 cm) high. It can have a hinged lid so that you can check on the young birds from time to time, or sliding glass and wood panels, as shown.

The shallow hollow in the base is to prevent the eggs from rolling around. If the birds roll any of the eggs out of the nesting box it means they are not fertilized and no babies can hatch out of them.

There is only space in this book to give a little information on breeding, but if you are seriously interested in raising young, there are other books that will tell you all you need to know (see page 31).

Best age to breed

Parakeets can mate at three to four months but it is best to wait until they are fully grown at 10 to 11 months before letting them rear a brood of chicks.

Mating

Pet parakeets can breed year-round. When in mating condition, the cock bird's cere becomes very bright blue and the hen's dark brown. You know parakeets are ready to mate when the cock begins to court the hen by singing to her while puffing up his head and throat feathers, and feeds her regurgitated food. They preen each other and rub beaks.

Egg-laying and incubation

After mating, the cock must be left with the hen, for her eggs will not mature inside her unless she can hear him singing. Also he will feed her while she is sitting on the eggs, and help to rear the brood.

Within two weeks of mating, the hen will lay her eggs. At this time the cage should be kept in a warm room and the air never allowed to get too dry.

Parakeet hens usually lay five or six eggs. They lay them one at a time, on every other day. Once she has begun to lay her eggs, a hen will sit on them to keep them warm and incubate them, hardly ever leaving the nesting box. Until the baby birds hatch, she relies on the cock to bring her food.

At 18 days the baby birds begin to hatch – one every other day, in the order in which the eggs were laid.

The baby parakeets

Baby budgies are born helpless and blind, and totally dependent on the parents to keep them warm under their feathers and feed them. But they develop quickly, and in four weeks they can already fly. At this age they begin to leave the nesting box, but they should stay with their parents for another two weeks.

Parakeets usually pair for life unless, of course, they are separated for some reason. These two are *pied* parakeets.

In the wild, baby parakeets have to be ready to fly with the flock when it migrates, so parakeet chicks develop quickly. At six days their eyes open, and at seven days their feathers begin to grow. After 10 days they are covered with down. At four weeks their wing and tail feathers are nearly fully grown.

Teaching your parakeet to talk

If you want your parakeet to talk you must start teaching it when it is very young, and be patient, because it may take several months to learn. Teaching sessions should last only 10 minutes, but they can be repeated as often as every two hours.

Begin by teaching your bird its name. Once it has learned to say this clearly, start to teach it other words – one at a time – and then short phrases. A good talker may manage quite long sentences after a while.

When teaching your parakeet to talk, hold it on your finger close to your face and repeat the word you want it to learn many times over. Do not shout, but speak loudly and distinctly, and always say the word in the same way. As with taming, only one person should try to teach a parakeet to talk. There should be nobody else in the room, and no distraction from a TV or radio.

Don't give up easily, but do not be disappointed if your bird does not respond – some parakeets can never be trained to talk.

Understanding your parakeet

How does a parakeet show it is happy?

A happy parakeet will eat well, sing, and generally be busy, either preening its feathers or playing with its toys.

How does a parakeet show it is afraid?

It may retreat into a corner of the cage, pull itself up tall and thin, or flutter around the cage. When its fright is over and it feels safe again, it often fluffs up its feathers and gives itself a good shake before it settles down.

How does it show it is pleased to see you?

It will hop towards you, and bob its head up and down. If it is on your shoulder it may preen your hair.

How does it behave when it wants to be left alone to sleep?

When it is ready to sleep, a parakeet retires to its favorite perch, fluffs up its feathers and perches on one leg, with the other drawn up under it. Often it buries its head in its feathers.

Your budgie may live to be 10 or even up to 18 years old. Throughout its life it will depend on you for everything it needs – it cannot look after itself and have the companionship of other birds as it would in the wild. So take good care of it, play with it, and make its life as interesting as possible. In return, it will give you a lot of fun and enjoyment.

Further reading

Parakeets, A Complete Pet Owner's Manual
Annette Wolter
Barron's, Hauppauge, NY, 1990

The New Parakeet Handbook
I. Birmelin / A. Wolter
Barron's, Hauppauge, NY, 1986
(very helpful on breeding)

The Complete Budgerigar
Matthew M. Vriends
Howell House, New York, 1985

Index